World Book, Inc.
233 N. Michigan Avenue
Chicago, IL 60601
U.S.A.

For information about other World Book publications,
visit our website at http://www.worldbookonline.com
or call 1-800-WORLDBK (967-5325).

For information about sales to schools and libraries, call
1-800-975-3250 (United States), or 1-800-837-5365 (Canada).

Staff

Executive Committee
President: Donald D. Keller
Vice President and Editor in Chief: Paul A. Kobasa
Vice President, Marketing/Digital Products: Sean Klunder
Vice President, International: Richard Flower
Controller: Yan Chen
Director, Human Resources: Bev Ecker

Editorial

Associate Director, Supplementary Publications:
  Scott Thomas
Managing Editor, Supplementary Publications:
  Barbara A. Mayes
Associate Manager, Supplementary Publications:
  Cassie Mayer
Editors: Brian Johnson and Kristina Vaicikonis
Researcher: Annie Brodsky
Editorial Assistant: Ethel Matthews
Manager, Contracts & Compliance
  (Rights & Permissions): Loranne K. Shields
Manager, Indexing: David Pofelski
Writer: David Alderton
Project Editor: Sarah Uttridge
Editorial Assistant: Kieron Connolly
Design: Andrew Easton

Graphics and Design

Senior Manager: Tom Evans
Senior Designer: Don Di Sante
Manager, Cartography: Wayne K. Pichler
Senior Cartographer: John Rejba

Pre-Press and Manufacturing

Director: Carma Fazio
Manufacturing Manager: Steven K. Hueppchen
Senior Production Manager: Janice Rossing
Production/Technology Manager: Anne Fritzinger
Proofreader: Emilie Schrage

Library of Congress Cataloging-in-Publication Data
Grasslands.
    p. cm. -- (Animals and their habitats)
   Summary: "This volume introduces many of the animal
  species that live in grasslands, prairies, and steppes. Special
  features include a glossary, photographs, an index, detailed
  captions describing each animal, and inset maps showing
  where on the globe the different species are found" --
  Provided by publisher.
   Includes index.
   ISBN 978-0-7166-0446-4
   1. Grassland animals--Juvenile literature. 2. Grassland
  ecology--Juvenile literature. I. World Book, Inc.
  QL115.3.G726 2012
  591.74--dc23
                        2012005836

Animals and Their Habitats
Set ISBN: 978-0-7166-0441-9

Printed in China by Leo Paper Products LTD.,
Heshan, Guangdong
1st printing July 2012

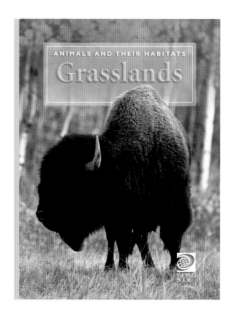

The American bison, often called a
buffalo, is one of many animals that
depend on the vast oceans of grass that
cover parts of every continent except
Antarctica. Many grassland animals are
under threat from overhunting and the
loss of their habitat to farming.

© Alamy (Juniors Bildarchiv)

Contents

Introduction

A vast sea of grass covers many areas of Earth, stretching from one horizon to the other. Most of these grasslands support few if any trees because relatively little rain falls. The climate can be extreme, with scorching heat in the day and bitter cold at night. Winters can be harsh. But grasslands provide a home for great herds of mammals and countless birds. The soil is filled with tunnels of rodents, which are eaten by snakes and other *predators* (hunting animals).

Grasslands cover many seasonal areas of our planet. They can be found throughout central North America. They stretch from southeastern Europe across much of Asia, into northeastern China. They also cover most of Argentina, in South America. Areas of Africa and Australia also have grasslands. In the United States, grasslands are often called prairies. In Russia, they are usually known as the steppes. In Argentina, grasslands are called the Pampas. But these areas all provide similar *habitat* (the type of place in which an animal lives).

The grasslands are home to mighty herds of such grazing animals as bison and saiga. The saiga's unusual nose helps it to cope with the climate of its grassland home, warming cold air in the winter and filtering out dust in the summer. Herding animals typically eat so much grass that they must often move to find food. Many follow the rains, especially in areas that have wet and dry seasons.

Such predators as wolves may follow the herds, picking off the younger and weaker animals. Living in herds offers protection, partly because the herd provides many sets of eyes to watch for predators. Herds can also close ranks to protect vulnerable young. Bulls may charge at predators, relying on their strength and sharp horns to drive away the hungry beasts.

EMU

SAIGA

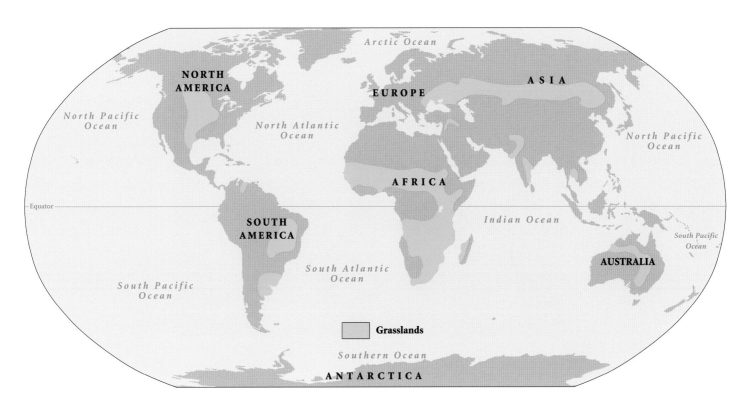

GRASSLANDS

GREAT GREEN BUSH CRICKET

Other animals hide from predators in the soil. Many rodents and similar animals build complex *burrows* (underground shelters), with many tunnels and rooms. But these burrows do not provide protection from all predators. Badgers can rip open burrows with their long claws. Snakes can slither inside.

Without trees, birds must hide their nests in the grass. They explode into the air when danger approaches. Other birds cannot fly at all. The emus of Australia can outrun their pursuers, reaching great speeds with their long legs. Grasslands provide an endless feast for birds of prey. They soar over the countryside, using their keen eyesight to spot prey on the ground. A hare may have no sense that it is in danger until it feels the grip of an eagle's claws.

American Bison

The American bison is often called a "buffalo" in the United States, but these animals are not closely related to true buffaloes. This species is the largest North American mammal.

VITAL STATISTICS

WEIGHT	Females 700–1,200 lb (318–544 kg); males 1,200–2,000 lb (544–907 kg)
LENGTH	Females 6–7 ft (1.8–2.1 m); males 9–13 ft (2.7–4.1 m)
SEXUAL MATURITY	4–5 years
LENGTH OF PREGNANCY	About 280 days
NUMBER OF OFFSPRING	1, though twins are recorded occasionally
DIET	Grasses, sedges, and similar plants
LIFE SPAN	Around 15 years in the wild; may live up to 25 in captivity

ANIMAL FACTS

Huge herds of American bison once thundered across the plains, but they were nearly wiped out by hunting during the 1800's. White American hunters killed millions of bison, partly to deprive Native Americans of a major food source. By the 1880's, there was a real risk that the American bison would become extinct. Today, the population has recovered to around 350,000 individuals. There were once more than 20 million.

WHERE IN THE WORLD?

Formerly ranged from northwestern to central Canada, and southward across most of the U.S. down into northern Mexico. Now largely confined to reserves.

HUMP
This raised area on the back consists of muscles attached to the bones of the spine. The muscles help support the bison's huge head. They also help the bison swing its head from side to side to clear away snow to find food in the winter.

HORNS
Both males and females have horns, but the horns on the males are usually wider, longer, and less curved.

COLORATION
Bison are usually brown or dark brown, but very rare white individuals born. They are considered sacred by many Native Americans.

BEARD
This is usually fuller on males.

A young American bison calf

HOW BIG IS IT?

TELLING THEM APART

The male bison has a much larger hump than the female, which is also smaller in overall size.

Saiga

VITAL STATISTICS

WEIGHT	66–99 lb (30–45 kg); males are heavier
LENGTH	3.2–4.9 ft (1–1.5 m), including tail; stands up to 2.6 ft (0.8 m) tall
SEXUAL MATURITY	Females 8 months; males about a year later
LENGTH OF PREGNANCY	140 days
NUMBER OF OFFSPRING	1 in the first litter, then 2; weaning at 120–160 days
DIET	Grazes on vegetation including grass, small plants, and lichens
LIFE SPAN	6–10 years

ANIMAL FACTS

The saiga's strange-looking inflatable nostrils act largely as a filter to remove dust during the summer. In winter, the nostrils help to warm the bitterly cold air before it passes into the lungs. Herds migrate north to better grazing in summer, heading back south to avoid the worst of the winter weather. The breeding season starts in the winter, and fights between males are often brutal. It is not unusual for males to die during these battles. One adult male breeds with a harem of many females.

The nostrils in cross-section

Since the 1990's, these unusual antelopes have become highly endangered, mainly because the males are poached for their horns. The horns are prized in traditional Chinese medicine.

WHERE IN THE WORLD?

From the Black Sea east through the grasslands of Russia into Kazakhstan, with a separate population in Mongolia.

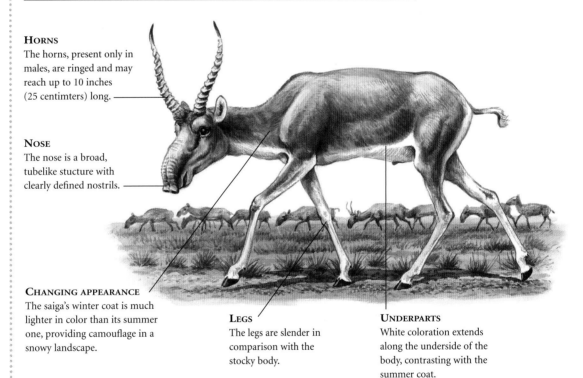

HORNS
The horns, present only in males, are ringed and may reach up to 10 inches (25 centimters) long.

NOSE
The nose is a broad, tubelike stucture with clearly defined nostrils.

CHANGING APPEARANCE
The saiga's winter coat is much lighter in color than its summer one, providing camouflage in a snowy landscape.

LEGS
The legs are slender in comparison with the stocky body.

UNDERPARTS
White coloration extends along the underside of the body, contrasting with the summer coat.

HOW BIG IS IT?

SYNCHRONIZED DELIVERY
Birthing is coordinated, so all females produce their calves within a short period. The birth of so many calves overwhelms *predators* (hunting animals) and allows more of the young to survive.

Pronghorn

VITAL STATISTICS

WEIGHT	88–132 lb (40–60 kg); females lighter on average
LENGTH	2.5–3.5 ft (0.8–1.0 m)
SEXUAL MATURITY	About 15 months, but males do not actually breed until they are 3 years old
LENGTH OF PREGNANCY	About 235 days; mating takes place in mid-September
NUMBER OF OFFSPRING	1
DIET	Eats flowering plants, shrubs, grasses, and cactuses
LIFE SPAN	10–15 years maximum

ANIMAL FACTS

The pronghorn is the fastest land mammal in North America—able to reach a speed of 60 miles (96 kilometers) per hour. This ability may have developed because it needed to outpace the now-extinct American cheetah, which hunted it. Although pronghorns look like antelopes, they are not closely related to antelopes or any other animal with horns and hoofs. Pronghorns are the only animal that sheds the *sheaths* (coverings) of their horns. They grow new sheaths every year.

Calves lie down in the grass to escape *predators* (hunting animals).

During the last ice age, at least a dozen species of pronghorns flourished in North America. Today, only one species of pronghorn remains.

WHERE IN THE WORLD?

Saskatchewan and Alberta in Canada, southwestern Minnesota and central Texas, extending west to northeastern California and south into Mexico. Also found in Baja California.

TAIL
The tail is short and white. When a pronghorn senses danger, it bristles the long hairs of its white rump to warn other pronghorns.

HORNS
The horns are eye-catching in males. The forward-pointing prongs account for their name.

EYES
The eyes are large and positioned high on the head, ensuring a good field of vision.

BUCKS AND DOES
Male pronghorns are called bucks. Female pronghorns are called does.

MALE MARKINGS
The black stripes running down the sides of the neck, along with the black mask on the face, are characteristic of male pronghorns.

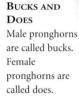

HOW BIG IS IT?

UNDER, NOT OVER
Pronghorns cannot jump well. Instead, they try to slip under ranchers' fences. They live in small groups in summer.

Maned Wolf

VITAL STATISTICS

WEIGHT	44–55 lb (20–25 kg)
LENGTH	5–5.5 ft (1.5–1.6 m); up to 3 ft (9 m) tall
SEXUAL MATURITY	2 years
LENGTH OF PREGNANCY	60–65 days
NUMBER OF OFFSPRING	2–6; weaning at around 105 days
DIET	Feeds on small animals, birds, and insects, but probably half of its diet consists of plant matter and fruit
LIFE SPAN	7–10 years in the wild; up to 15 in captivity

These distinctive animals are the largest member of the dog family living in South America. Despite their name, they are not true wolves.

WHERE IN THE WORLD?

Lives in southern South America, in central and southeastern parts of Brazil, plus eastern Paraguay and Bolivia. Also found in northern Argentina.

ANIMAL FACTS

Maned wolves are active at night. They rely on their keen senses of smell and hearing to locate prey hidden in the grass. During the day, they rest in heavy brush. Maned wolves do not live in *packs* (groups). Instead, male and female pairs occupy *territories* (home areas) of up to 11.5 square miles (30 square kilometers). However, even within the same territory, the male and female live apart. Maned wolves are not true wolves. They look like foxes, but they are not true foxes either. Rather, they are unique members of the dog family.

The maned wolf has a very narrow body.

TAIL
The tail can be completely white or have white fur just at the tip.

MANE
This ridge of fur can be raised and extends from the neck down over the shoulders.

EARS
The ears may reach up to 7 inches (18 centimeters) long and help to locate prey hidden in grass.

LEGS
Long and relatively slender, the legs emphasize the athletic nature of this canine.

CAT IN WOLF'S CLOTHING?
The maned wolf pounces on rodents from above. This is similar to the way cats hunt rodents.

HOW BIG IS IT?

Gray Wolf

SPECIES • *Canis lupus*

Wolves once lived throughout much of the Northern Hemisphere, but people have destroyed large numbers of them. Despite their reputation for being dangerous, wolves usually avoid human beings.

VITAL STATISTICS

WEIGHT	35–175 lb (15–80 kg); males and northern wolves are heavier
LENGTH	3–4 ft (0.9–1.3 m); up to 2.8 ft (0.9 m) tall
SEXUAL MATURITY	2–3 years
LENGTH OF PREGNANCY	60–63 days
NUMBER OF OFFSPRING	1–19, average 5–6; weaned by 70 days
DIET	Hunts such mammals as bison, deer, sheep, goats, and caribou
LIFE SPAN	6–9 years; may live over 12 years in captivity

ANIMAL FACTS

Wolves live in family groups called packs, with 8 to 20 members. Packs may work together to take down such large prey as moose. Packs claim a specific home area called a territory, which they defend against other wolves and competitors such as coyotes. Dogs were *domesticated* (tamed) from wolves, perhaps more than 30,000 years ago, longer than any other animal.

Wolf

Dog

Domestic dogs are directly descended from wolves.

WHERE IN THE WORLD?

Ranges across northern North America and northern Asia. Small numbers live in Europe, India, and the Middle East.

MUZZLE
Male gray wolves have broader muzzles and foreheads than females do.

COLORATION
Despite its name, the gray wolf's coat color is actually a mix of colors.

COAT STRUCTURE
The coat is double-layered, with a weather-resistant outer layer and an insulating undercoat.

PACK ORDER
Each wolf pack has a social order called a dominance hierarchy. Packs are ruled by a breeding pair. Other members of the pack help to raise the cubs but usually do not breed themselves.

HOW BIG IS IT?

FEET
Slight webbing between the toes helps wolves walk over snowy ground without sinking into it.

Bat-Eared Fox

These small foxes eat mostly insects, especially dung beetles and termites. The name of the bat-eared fox refers to its large, sensitive ears, which help it to find insects at night.

VITAL STATISTICS

WEIGHT	7–10 lb (3–4.5 kg); males are slightly larger
LENGTH	1.5–2 ft (0.5–0.6 m); up to 1.3 ft (.4 m) tall
SEXUAL MATURITY	8–9 months
LENGTH OF PREGNANCY	About 60 days
NUMBER OF OFFSPRING	2–5; weaning occurs at 5 weeks
DIET	Eats mostly insects and similar animals; also feeds on small mammals, lizards, and birds
LIFE SPAN	4–6 years in the wild; up to 13 in captivity

ANIMAL FACTS

Living in pairs, these foxes inhabit areas of grassland and scrubland. They often follow herds of grazing animals to feed on dung beetles, which eat solid animal waste. The foxes look rather like small jackals. They are often killed for this reason, though they pose no threat to such *domesticated* (tamed) livestock as sheep. The female gives birth at the start of the rainy season, when insect prey is likely to be most abundant. The young leave the den for the first time when they are about two weeks old. Adults breed just once a year.

WHERE IN THE WORLD?

Occurs in two populations, one in eastern Africa, and the other in southern Africa.

FUR COLOR
The fur is grayish-brown, broken up with lighter yellowish areas, especially around the throat.

EARS
The ears reach about 5 inches (13 centimeters) long and are quite broad. They help to locate prey at night.

FRONT PAWS
The front paws are often used for digging a den or helping to catch prey.

LEGS
The legs are a dark shade of brown.

DANGEROUS LIVING

The small size of these foxes means they are vulnerable not just to hyenas and other ground *predators* (hunting animals) but also birds of prey.

HOW BIG IS IT?

Bobcat

VITAL STATISTICS

WEIGHT	15–31 lb (7–14 kg); males are heavier
LENGTH	2.5–4 ft (0.7–1.2 m), including tail; about 1.3 ft (0.4 m) tall
SEXUAL MATURITY	1–2 years
LENGTH OF PREGNANCY	About 63-70 days
NUMBER OF OFFSPRING	Average 2–4, but can be up to 6; weaning occurs at around 60 days
DIET	Hunts a variety of small animals, especially rabbits
LIFE SPAN	Up to 16 years; double this in captivity

ANIMAL FACTS

Bobcats live in a wide variety of *habitats* (places), including forests, grasslands, scrublands, swamps, and even the fringes of cities. Their diet ranges from insects to small deer. They are stealthy hunters that stalk their prey and then pounce, killing with a bite to the neck. Bobcats live on their own, marking their *territories* (home areas) with scent and scratches on trees. A successful male's territory overlaps with those of several females. But the sexes do not mix, except during the breeding season.

The eyes of bobcats (left) are more yellow than those of other wildcats (right).

Unlike many wildcats, the bobcat has a short tail. This short tail probably reflects the cat's preference for life on the ground rather than in the trees, as a long tail helps to provide balance.

WHERE IN THE WORLD?

Ranges from southern Canada down through much of the United States, into Baja California and most of Mexico.

TAIL
The bobcat is named for its short tail, which resembles a bob, or knob. The tail measures just 4 inches (10 centimeters) long and has a white underside.

EARS
The ears are tall and pointed, with small black tufts of hair at the tips.

COLORATION
Background color can vary from grayish-brown to tan; the spotted patterning is highly individual.

LEGS
The hind legs are longer than the front legs, which explains this cat's characteristic bobbing gait.

HOW BIG IS IT?

SHARP TALK
Scratching in this way sharpens the bobcat's claws and leaves a visual marker of its territory, which is defined by its scent.

Jaguarundi

VITAL STATISTICS

WEIGHT	From 11–22 lb (5–10 kg)
LENGTH	3–4 ft (0.9–1.2 m), including tail; up to 1 ft (0.3 m) tall
SEXUAL MATURITY	About 24 months
LENGTH OF PREGNANCY	70-75 days
NUMBER OF OFFSPRING	Average 1–4, but can be up to 5; weaning occurs at 42 days
DIET	Hunts rodents, birds including domestic chickens, as well as frogs and fish
LIFE SPAN	Up to 15 years

ANIMAL FACTS

Scientists once thought that jaguarundis belonged to two separate species. Later, they learned that grayish and reddish jaguarundis do breed. In fact, both types may be born in a single litter. This cat often spends time in the trees. It becomes active in the evening, when it descends to the ground to hunt. Farmers sometimes kill jaguarundis because the animals may feed on chickens. Jaguarundis are also caught in traps meant for other animals. But they are not considered threatened.

Jaguarundis are fast and graceful.

This cat is sometimes called the otter cat because of its unusual appearance. Jaguarundis come in two colors—grayish-black and russet-red. The reddish cats are sometimes known as eyra.

WHERE IN THE WORLD?

Range extends from the southern United States through Central and South America to northern Argentina. Has been introduced to Florida.

HEAD
The head is slender, with small ears, rounded at their tips.

COLORATION
A grayish-black jaguarundi is seen here. The young may be spotted at birth.

LEGS
Although short, the legs are powerful, and the feet are equipped with strong claws.

TAIL
The tail is quite long, reaching 24 inches (61 centimeters).

DIFFERENT COLORS

Two separate color variations exist—grayish-black and russet-red. The depth of coloration varies between individuals.

HOW BIG IS IT?

American Badger

SPECIES • *Taxidea taxus*

VITAL STATISTICS

WEIGHT	9–25 lb (4–12 kg); males are heavier
LENGTH	2–3 ft (0.5–0.9 m)
SEXUAL MATURITY	Females 4 months; males 2 years
LENGTH OF PREGNANCY	40-42 days; development starts about 6 months after mating
NUMBER OF OFFSPRING	1–5, but averages 3; weaning occurs at 12 weeks
DIET	Hunts small animals, including insects, ground-nesting birds, and rodents; also eats some plant matter
LIFE SPAN	4–14 years in the wild; up to 26 in captivity

American badgers are known for their ferocity. Adult badgers are rarely attacked by other animals, because of their sharp claws, unpleasant odor, and aggressive nature.

WHERE IN THE WORLD?

Lives in central and western North America, from the grasslands of the Midwest to the Pacific Coast, up through southern Canada.

ANIMAL FACTS

American badgers are superb diggers because of their large claws, which can reach 2 inches (5 centimeters) long. Badgers move regularly between different dens in their *territory* (home area). They defend themselves with their claws and by releasing an unpleasant, musky scent. They sometimes team up with coyotes to hunt rodents. The badgers dig well but run slowly, while coyotes are fast but do not dig well. When they work together, few rodents can escape.

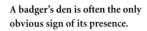

A badger's den is often the only obvious sign of its presence.

FACE
The face is triangular, with a long nose that points upwards at the tip. The ears are small.

FRONT PAWS
The front paws are strong, with long, curved claws ending in sharp points.

TAIL
The tail is short and stocky and thickly covered in fur.

COLORATION
Silvery-brown over much of the body, with a white stripe extending back over the shoulders from the nose.

HOW BIG IS IT?

STAYING SNUG
American badgers are able to escape the worst of the harsh winter weather by sleeping below ground in their dens. But they awaken easily and may venture out on warm winter days.

Giant Anteater

The largest of the anteaters, this species lives in relatively open countryside and relies on its amazingly long tongue and powerful claws to feed on ants and termites.

VITAL STATISTICS

WEIGHT	40–140 lb (18–64 kg); males are bigger
LENGTH	Up to 6 ft (1.8 m) including tail
SEXUAL MATURITY	2.5–4 years
LENGTH OF PREGNANCY	190 days; mother gives birth standing up, using her tail for support
NUMBER OF OFFSPRING	1, sometimes 2; weaning occurs at about 6 months
DIET	Feeds on ants and termites, but it avoids fierce army ants
LIFE SPAN	Up to 15 years in the wild; 26 years in captivity

ANIMAL FACTS

Giant anteaters tend to spend more time on the ground than their smaller relatives, though they still climb well. They are also good swimmers. Individuals occupy large *territories* (home areas), with many insect nests for them to plunder. An anteater can eat more than 30,000 ants a day. Unfortunately, giant anteaters are threatened by hunting and the destruction of their *habitat* (area where an animal lives), and they have disappeared from most of Central America.

The anteater's sharp front claws can rip apart ant or termite nests.

WHERE IN THE WORLD?

Ranges from Panama in Central America through South America to the east of the Andes, as far south as northern parts of Argentina and Uruguay.

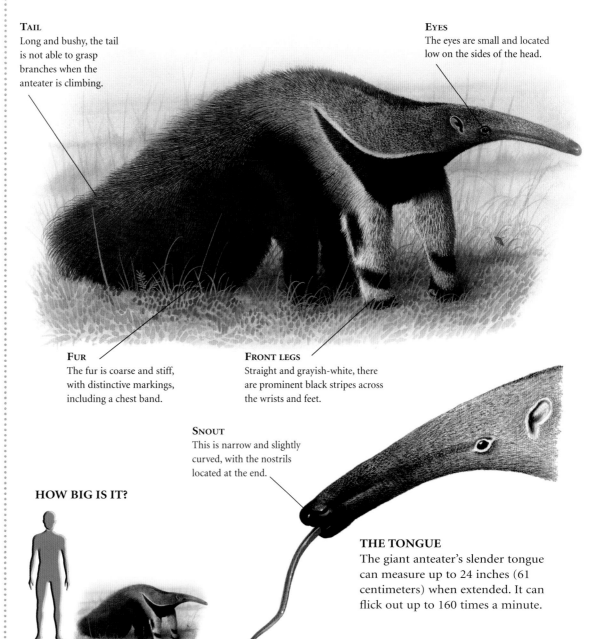

TAIL
Long and bushy, the tail is not able to grasp branches when the anteater is climbing.

EYES
The eyes are small and located low on the sides of the head.

FUR
The fur is coarse and stiff, with distinctive markings, including a chest band.

FRONT LEGS
Straight and grayish-white, there are prominent black stripes across the wrists and feet.

SNOUT
This is narrow and slightly curved, with the nostrils located at the end.

HOW BIG IS IT?

THE TONGUE
The giant anteater's slender tongue can measure up to 24 inches (61 centimeters) when extended. It can flick out up to 160 times a minute.

Indian Rhinoceros

SPECIES • *Rhinoceros unicornis*

The Indian rhinoceros was nearly wiped out by hunting. Poachers continue to kill them for their horns, which are used in traditional Chinese medicine. Fewer than 3,000 individuals survive today.

VITAL STATISTICS

WEIGHT	4,000–6,000 lb (1,800–2,700 kg); males are bigger
LENGTH	11–12 ft (3.3–4.2 m); up to 6 ft (1.8 m) tall at the shoulder
SEXUAL MATURITY	Females 5–6 years; males 9 years
LENGTH OF PREGNANCY	16–18 months; females give birth once every 3 years
NUMBER OF OFFSPRING	1; weaning occurs at 18 months
DIET	Grazes on grasses, leaves, branches, and water plants
LIFE SPAN	Up to 45 years

WHERE IN THE WORLD?

Their range once extended from Pakistan as far east as China, but these rhinos are now confined to Nepal and northeastern India, in the Himalayan foothills.

ANIMAL FACTS

The Indian rhinoceros lives in tall grasslands and open forests, where it can hide. The animal can move surprisingly fast, at speeds of up to 35 miles (56 kilometers) per hour. The rhinoceros is now confined to national parks and other protected areas. Their numbers have begun to recover thanks to strict antipoaching measures. One group of rhinos in Nepal is protected by hundreds of armed rangers. But the animals remain threatened by poaching and destruction of their *habitat* (area).

A series of ridges covers the back and sides of the body.

HORN
A single, relatively short horn grows on the head.

SKIN
The hairless skin is brownish-gray. It forms a series of plates that look as if they are joined by rivets.

LEGS AND FEET
The legs are stumpy, and there are three toes on each foot.

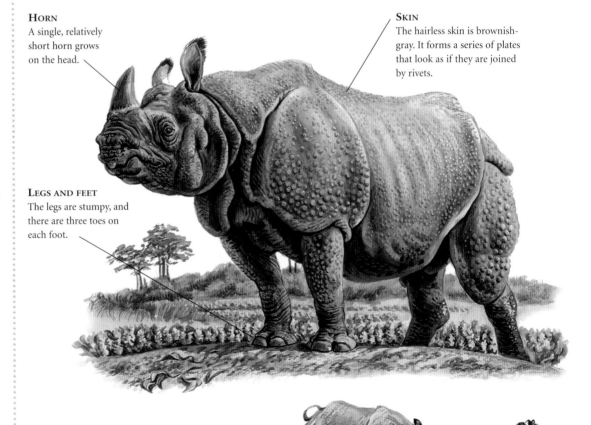

HOW BIG IS IT?

DEFENSIVE STRATEGY
Adult Indian rhinoceroses are unlikely to be attacked, but their calves can be vulnerable to tigers. The female defends her calf by charging repeatedly.

European Mole

VITAL STATISTICS

WEIGHT	0.2–0.3 lb (0.1 kg); males slightly bigger
LENGTH	0.5–1 ft (0.14–0.2 m) overall; tail is about a quarter of the body length
SEXUAL MATURITY	About 1 year
LENGTH OF PREGNANCY	33 days;. 1 litter a year; breeds March–May
NUMBER OF OFFSPRING	2–7, average 3; weaning occurs at 30 days
DIET	Eats mainly earthworms and insects
LIFE SPAN	Up to 5 years

ANIMAL FACTS

Moles thrive in grasslands with soils that are good for tunneling. Their *burrows* (underground shelters) are large and complex, with many tunnels and rooms, including sleeping chambers and nests. In areas with clay soils, moles may live in the same tunnels for generations. These animals spend most of their waking hours digging for earthworms and insects. The animals are highly territorial, especially the males. During the breeding season, males may dig long tunnels in search of females. In certain areas, including gardens and ranches, people may kill moles to prevent damage caused by the tunnels.

European moles are skilled diggers that hardly ever come to the surface. However, moles give away their presence by creating small mounds of soil known as molehills.

WHERE IN THE WORLD?

Lives in western and central Europe, but is absent from Ireland and southern areas such as Italy. Extends east into parts of Russia.

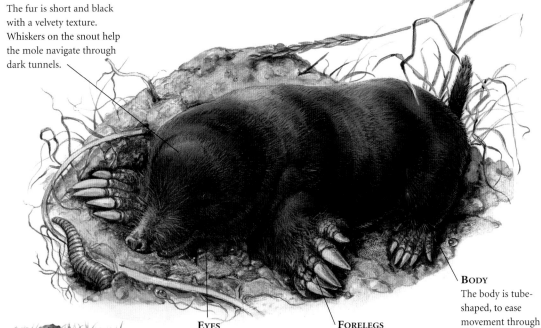

COAT
The fur is short and black with a velvety texture. Whiskers on the snout help the mole navigate through dark tunnels.

BODY
The body is tube-shaped, to ease movement through tunnels.

EYES
Eyes are small because moles cannot rely on vision in their dark tunnels.

FORELEGS
Large and shovellike, these are turned outwards and equipped with five claws.

MOLEHILLS
Moles push soil up into small mounds known as molehills.

TUNNEL SYSTEMS
The mole's underground burrows are large. Females create snug nests, where the young are born.

HOW BIG IS IT?

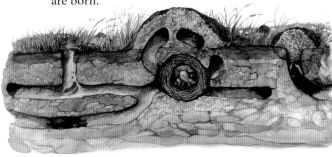

Snowshoe Hare

VITAL STATISTICS

WEIGHT	2–4 lb (0.9–1.8 kg)
LENGTH	1.3–1.7 ft (0.4–0.5 m)
SEXUAL MATURITY	1 year
LENGTH OF PREGNANCY	36–40 days; breeds from mid-March to August
NUMBER OF OFFSPRING	1–7, typically 3; weaning occurs by 28 days; females may have up to 4 litters per year
DIET	Eats grass, herbs, and bark
LIFE SPAN	Up to 5 years

ANIMAL FACTS

In many areas, the numbers of these hares follows a boom-and-bust cycle. Their population builds up over time, as do those of the animals that feed on them. Then, the hare's numbers crash, which causes a similar crash of *predators* (hunting animals). During the boom, there can be as many as 10,000 hares per square mile (2.6 square kilometers). This cycle is caused in part by the smaller number of *species* (kinds) that live in northern areas. As a result, predators have fewer other species to rely on if the numbers of one these species drop dramatically.

There is great contrast between the winter coat (left) and summer coat (right).

The name of these hares refers to their large feet, which help them to run quickly on soft snow. They change color from brown to white as winter approaches, helping them to blend into a snowy landscape.

WHERE IN THE WORLD?

Lives across northern North America to as far south as New Mexico, around the Great Lakes and reaching North Carolina in the east.

EYES
It is hard to approach a snowshoe hare without being noticed, as they have a wide field of vision.

EARS
The large ears of these hares can turn to listen for danger.

CHANGING CAMOUFLAGE
The hares shed and replace their fur twice a year as the seasons change.

HIND FEET
Large and well-covered by fur, these enable the hare to run easily over the snow.

HOW BIG IS IT?

DANGEROUS LIVING
Snowshoe hares face many dangers, but they can run and jump well, covering up to 10 feet (3 meters) in a single bound.

European Hare

SPECIES • *Lepus europaeus*

European hares have sharp vision and hearing to help them detect danger. They can run at speeds of up to 35 miles (60 kilometers) per hour, changing direction frequently to escape pursuers.

VITAL STATISTICS

WEIGHT	6.5–11 lb (3–5 kg)
LENGTH	2–2.5 ft (0.6–0.8 m)
SEXUAL MATURITY	8 months
LENGTH OF PREGNANCY	30–40 days; breeds in late winter and mid-summer
NUMBER OF OFFSPRING	1–8, typically 4; weaning at 30 days; females may have 2–4 litters per year
DIET	Eats grass, herbs and twigs; can be a crop pest
LIFE SPAN	Up to 10 years

ANIMAL FACTS

Unlike many other grassland mammals, hares do not live in *burrows* (underground shelters). Instead, they rest in hollows on the ground. The female hides her offspring in different spots, rather than risk having them all killed by one hungry animal. The mother then makes rounds to nurse them. A female can have up to seven litters of young each year, and the hares can quickly increase in numbers. However, their numbers are usually controlled by coyotes, foxes, wolves, wildcats, and birds of prey. In Argentina and Australia, the hares have become pests.

Hares rely on speed and maneuverability to escape danger.

WHERE IN THE WORLD?

Lives across Europe, including the British Isles, the Arabian Peninsula, and into Asia. Introduced elsewhere, including North America, Argentina, and Australia.

COLORATION
Color can vary from yellowish-brown to grayish-brown, with the coat becoming grayer in winter.

EARS
These reach 4 inches (10 centimeters) long and have black tips.

THE LIP
extends up from the base of the upper lip and divides around the base of the nose.

HOW BIG IS IT?

THE "MAD MARCH" HARE

Hares may run around wildly during the height of breeding in March. This behavior may explain the phrase "mad as a March hare." Males sometimes fight one another for access to females.

Mara

The mara is sometimes known as the Patagonian hare because of its rabbitlike ears and the way it runs. But the mara is actually a large rodent. It is a close relative of the guinea pig.

VITAL STATISTICS

WEIGHT	17.5–35 lb (8–16 kg)
LENGTH	2.5–3 ft (0.7–0.8 m)
SEXUAL MATURITY	Around 6 months for both sexes
LENGTH OF PREGNANCY	90–98 days
NUMBER OF OFFSPRING	1–3; weaning occurs after about 60 days
DIET	Mainly grass and herbs, clipping them with their sharp *incisor* (cutting) teeth
LIFE SPAN	5–7 years; up to 15 in captivity

ANIMAL FACTS

Maras escape from *predators* (hunting animals) by running quickly, reaching a top speed of 28 miles (45 kilometers) per hour over short distances. They also can hop like rabbits. Males and females usually pair for life. Males fiercely guard their mates from other males. Females provide most of the care to offspring. But males contribute by watching for predators. The numbers of these rodents is falling, mainly because of the destruction of their *habitat* (area) and competition with sheep.

WHERE IN THE WORLD?

Lives in South America, in the Pampas of central and southern Argentina.

BODY SHAPE
Unlike most rodents, maras are athletic, and adults can often outrun predators.

HEAD
Keen hearing and large eyes help alert these rodents to danger.

LEGS
These are long and slender, with four sharp claws on each front foot and three behind.

COLORATION
Upperparts of the body are gray, becoming chestnut on the sides of the face and underparts.

A SHARED DEN

Mara usually live as pairs, but the offspring of many different maras may share a den. However, only one pair of adults visits the den at a time.

Pairs are constantly alert to danger but may sit down to graze.

HOW BIG IS IT?

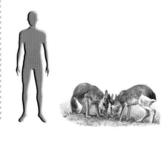

Guinea Pig

SPECIES • *Cavia aperea*

Pet guinea pigs were *domesticated* (tamed) from this species several thousand years ago, originally as a food source. The wild species is sometimes known as the Brazilian guinea pig.

VITAL STATISTICS

WEIGHT	About 1.1–1.7 lb (0.5–0.8 kg)
LENGTH	1.1 ft (0.4 m)
SEXUAL MATURITY	74–77 days; females mature slightly earlier than males
LENGTH OF PREGNANCY	63–68 days
NUMBER OF OFFSPRING	2–3, normally weaned after 3–4 weeks
DIET	Grass and herbs
LIFE SPAN	Up to 6 years

WHERE IN THE WORLD?

Found in South America, east of the Andes in Colombia, Ecuador, Paraguay, Brazil, Argentina, and Uruguay.

ANIMAL FACTS

These animals live in grasslands as well as open highlands, at elevations up to nearly 10,000 feet (3,000 meters). They are social by nature and make chattering noises to keep in touch with one another out in the open. When threatened, an individual guinea pig freezes, in the hope that a *predator* (hunting animal) will not be able to spot it. A group of guinea pigs will scatter, to confuse predators and allow most members of the group to esape. Guinea pigs are most active at dawn and dusk. Whenever possible, they hide in dense grass or under rocks. However, they do not dig *burrows* (underground shelters).

Young look like miniature adults and are born with their eyes open.

COLORATION
Different breeds of guinea pigs have different colors, but their ancestors had short brownish fur.

EARS
These are broad and relatively short. Guinea pigs have good hearing.

PROFILE
The body curves down over the rump. Guinea pigs have no tail.

HINDQUARTERS
These are well-muscled, helping guinea pigs to run fast across the ground.

DANGER OVERHEAD
Guinea pigs that live in open areas are especially vulnerable to birds of prey.

HOW BIG IS IT?

Meadow Vole

VITAL STATISTICS

WEIGHT	1–2.5 oz (33–65 g)
LENGTH	About 5 in (13 cm) overall; tail is less than half body length
SEXUAL MATURITY	Females from 25 days; males from 45 days
LENGTH OF PREGNANCY	21 days; up to 17 litters a year recorded
NUMBER OF OFFSPRING	6–7, but can range from 2–9; weaning at 14 days
DIET	Grasses, herbs, seeds, fruit, even bark and dead animal matter
LIFE SPAN	1 year

The meadow vole is a very adaptable and common species and ranks as the most widely distributed member of its group in North America.

WHERE IN THE WORLD?

Range extends through much of North America north of Mexico and the Gulf Coast.

ANIMAL FACTS

Female meadow voles can produce litters constantly for most of the year. This enables voles to increase in number quickly. However, their lives are usually hazardous and short, as they face many *predators* (hunting animals), including birds of prey, foxes, and snakes. When a vole detects a predator, it may try to reach its *burrow* (underground shelter) or just freeze in place to try to escape detection.

Meadow voles may strip the bark from trees for food in the winter, an action that may damage the trees.

EARS
These may be small and relatively hard to see, but these voles have keen hearing.

COLORATION
Blackish-brown upperparts, often with a reddish hue, and paler underparts.

FEET
The toes on each foot have sharp, pointed claws.

HEARTY EATERS
Meadow voles can eat up to 60 percent of their body weight each day.

HOW BIG IS IT?

TUNNELING
Meadow voles construct burrows with various entrances that expand into chambers, where they rear their young and hide.

Botta's Pocket Gopher

SPECIES • *Thomomys bottae*

These rodents live mainly underground in a network of tunnels. They use the pouches in their cheeks to carry food back to their burrows, which have special chambers for storing food.

VITAL STATISTICS

WEIGHT	4–9 oz (120–250 g); males are slightly larger
LENGTH	9–10 in (22–26 cm)
SEXUAL MATURITY	9–10 months
LENGTH OF PREGNANCY	Around 19 days
NUMBER OF OFFSPRING	3–7, typically 6; weaning occurs at 36–40 days, and the young disperse at 2 months
DIET	Eats roots, bulbs, and other plant matter; may cause damage to crops
LIFE SPAN	Around 2.5 years

ANIMAL FACTS

These rodents spend their lives underground, in *habitats* (areas) ranging from grasslands to deserts. They are able to construct burrows in many types of soil, including heavy clay. The gophers usually come up to the surface only when the ground is covered with snow. They create tunnels in the snow, which they may line with soil. Unlike moles, gophers do not push up mounds of soil above their tunnels. Instead, they pile up the soil around the entrances to their burrows. Nests within the burrows are lined with dry grass. Chambers used to store food are not lined with grass.

WHERE IN THE WORLD?

Found in western North America, from Oregon south to Baja California, extending east into Texas and central Mexico.

TEETH
The *incisor* (cutting) teeth at the front of the mouth are sharp and can inflict a painful bite.

COLORATION
Variable, but reflects the soil where the gophers live.

FRONT FEET
These are short, yet powerful, equipped with sharp claws for digging.

CHEEK POUCHES
These animals are known as pocket gophers because of their cheek pouches. These fur-lined pockets, which extend from the sides of the mouth to beyond the shoulders, are used to carry food.

DANGERS OUTSIDE THE BURROW
Individuals are territorial and live alone. Out in the open, they are vulnerable to many *predators* (hunting animals), including birds of prey.

HOW BIG IS IT?

NETWORK OF BURROWS
These rodents dig a complicated series of interconnecting rooms and tunnels. These may extend over 492 feet (150 meters).

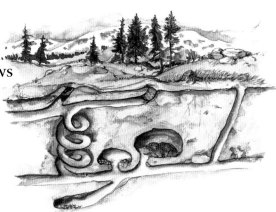

Eurasian Harvest Mouse

SPECIES • *Micromys minutus*

VITAL STATISTICS

WEIGHT	0.2 oz (6 g)
LENGTH	2–3 in (6 cm) overall; tail is similar length to the body
SEXUAL MATURITY	6 weeks
LENGTH OF PREGNANCY	17–19 days; 3 litters a year
NUMBER OF OFFSPRING	1–7; weaning occurs around 16 days
DIET	Seeds, bulbs and fruit, but insects may be eaten in summer, along with fungi and moss
LIFE SPAN	12–18 months

ANIMAL FACTS

Harvest mice are most active around dusk, which is why they have relatively large eyes. They are most visible in the summer, when they sleep above the ground in ball-shaped nests. During winter, they prefer to tunnel away and keep a store of food in a *burrow* (underground shelter). Their habit of nesting in fields of grain has led to a drop in their numbers in some areas, because their nests are destroyed by harvesting machines. But their numbers remain healthy overall.

Mothers may carry their young in their mouths.

The Eurasian harvest mouse is the smallest European rodent. Its tail is able to grasp plant stems, freeing its front paws to collect food.

WHERE IN THE WORLD?

Lives in Europe, south of Scandinavia, and only in southern parts of the British Isles. Extends across Asia, from Russia to Korea, and south into China.

A HELPING HAND
The harvest mouse is the only European rodent with a grasping tail.

EYES
Black and quite striking, these are located close to the muzzle.

COLORATION
Yellowish-brown on the upperparts with white underparts.

FEET
These allow the mouse to climb easily.

TAIL
The pink tail is largely free of hair.

HOW BIG IS IT?

ALTERNATIVE LIFESTYLES
Harvest mice weave blades of grass into ball-shaped nests 2 ½ to 7 inches (6 to 18 centimeters) in diameter. The mice may build their nests above ground on stems of grass or in the branches of a bush. They also may nest on the ground.

Black-Tailed Prairie Dog

SPECIES • *Cynomys ludovicianus*

VITAL STATISTICS

WEIGHT	2–3 lb (0.9–1.4 kg); males are often bigger
LENGTH	1.4–1.8 ft (0.43–0.53 m)
SEXUAL MATURITY	1–2 years
LENGTH OF PREGNANCY	28–35 days; 1 litter a year
NUMBER OF OFFSPRING	3–5, but can be up to 8; weaning by 49 days
DIET	Mainly grass, as well as herbs; also eats grasshoppers and other insects
LIFE SPAN	3–5 years

ANIMAL FACTS

Prairie-dog towns are made up of tunnels and nests that can cover a vast area of land. They are so extensive that the towns are divided into "neighborhoods" made up of the homes of many related females and one or two males. Studies suggest that many *species* (types) of plants and animals benefit from the presence of prairie dogs. Among these are the endangered black-footed ferret, which preys on the rodents. Since the 1800's, prairie dog populations have dropped dramatically because of hunting, the destruction of their *habitat* (living area), and an infectious disease called plague.

Prairie dogs rarely stray far from the protection of their tunnels.

Black-tailed prairie dogs are highly social. They live in large colonies known as prairie-dog towns. One town in Texas in the 1800's may have contained an estimated 400 million prairie dogs.

WHERE IN THE WORLD?

Lives throughout the western Great Plains of North America, from south-central Canada south to northeastern Mexico.

WHAT'S IN A NAME?
The animal gets its name from the *prairies* (grassy plains) where it lives, and from its warning call, which sounds like a domestic dog's bark.

SOUND AND SIGHT
Prairie dogs have very keen hearing and good eyesight.

COLORATION
Individuals range from shades of gray to brown and black.

SITTING
This upright posture enables prairie dogs to spot danger and escape.

HOW BIG IS IT?

GREETING
Touching the front teeth in this way is described as "kissing." It serves as a greeting between family members.

European Ground Squirrel

SPECIES • *Spermophilus citellus*

The European ground squirrel lives in *burrows* (underground shelters) rather than trees. It requires open country and does not live in areas with high grasses. It is also known as the European souslik.

VITAL STATISTICS

WEIGHT	0.5–1 lb (0.2–0.4 kg); builds up fat reserves in autumn
LENGTH	9.5–12 in (24–30 cm)
SEXUAL MATURITY	11 months
LENGTH OF PREGNANCY	27 days; 1 litter a year
NUMBER OF OFFSPRING	5–8, average 6; weaning occurs at 30–34 days
DIET	Nuts, seeds, and plant matter including herbs; also some small animals and bird eggs
LIFE SPAN	Up to 7 years

ANIMAL FACTS

These ground squirrels live close together, but individuals have their own burrows. They may occupy short-term dens, where they retreat on occasion during the day. They also have deeper burrows that are used for *hibernation* (sleeplike state) over the winter. The entrance to the den will be blocked off, with a side tunnel connecting to the surface through which the squirrels can emerge in the spring. The number of these squirrels is in serious decline, mainly because of the destruction of their *habitat* (living area) for agriculture.

WHERE IN THE WORLD?

Found in central and southeastern Europe, as far east as Ukraine.

FACIAL FEATURES
The forehead is long and relatively flat. The dark eyes are large but the ears are small.

COLORATION
Yellowish-gray along the back, with much paler underparts.

FORELEGS
These can act as paws to hold food and are used to dig burrows.

TAIL
This is about one-third the length of the body and is covered in hair.

STOCKING UP
Although these ground squirrels may take hay and food underground, they do not store food to eat over the winter.

HIBERNATION
Males start to hibernate before females, as early as August. They are not seen above ground until March.

HOW BIG IS IT?

Cattle Egret

VITAL STATISTICS

WEIGHT	9.5–18.3 oz (270–520 g)
LENGTH	18.1–22.0 in (46–56 cm)
WINGSPAN	34.6–37.8 in (88–96 cm)
NUMBER OF EGGS	2–5 eggs
INCUBATION PERIOD	22–26 days
NUMBER OF BROODS	1 a year
TYPICAL DIET	Insects, spiders, earthworms, amphibians, lizards
LIFE SPAN	Up to 15 years

This bird is often observed feeding near herds of cattle, but it also associates with many other animals that feed on grass, including wild buffalo, rhinos, elephants, hippos, zebras, giraffes, and waterbucks.

WHERE IN THE WORLD?

Native to southern Spain and northwestern Africa, it has spread to North and South America, most of Africa, Southeast Asia, eastern Australia, and New Zealand.

ANIMAL FACTS

The cattle egret feeds near grazing animals because the herds disturb many insects as they move. As the insects flee, the cattle egret snaps them up with its long bill. The cattle egret is usually white, with a yellow bill and legs. The large feet are black. During the breeding season, buff-colored plumes develop on the head, breast, and back. The bill, legs, and eyes also become reddish. Males tend to be larger than females.

HEAD
The head is rounded and sits on a neck that is longer than the neck of most other egrets.

BILL
The bill is large and is well suited to snatching insects from the grass.

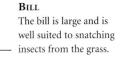

WINGS
The large, wide wings make the cattle egret slow in flight, but they allow it to soar on *thermals* (rising air currents).

GLOBE TROTTER
Until the mid-1800's, this bird lived chiefly in Africa. As cattle ranching has spread around the world, the cattle egret has spread with it. It now inhabits every continent except Antarctica.

Cattle egret

HOW BIG IS IT?

FANCY DRESS
During the mating season, the birds develop brownish-tan plumes on their head and chest, and their beak becomes orange.

Eastern Imperial Eagle

SPECIES · *Aquila heliaca*

VITAL STATISTICS

WEIGHT	About 6.6 lb (3 kg)
LENGTH	27.5–32.7 in (70–83 cm)
WINGSPAN	5.6–6.6 ft (1.7–2 m)
SEXUAL MATURITY	At least 4 years
LAYS EGGS	March–April
INCUBATION PERIOD	43–44 days
FLEDGLING PERIOD	60–77 days
NUMBER OF EGGS	2 eggs
NUMBER OF BROODS	1 a year
TYPICAL DIET	Mammals and birds
LIFESPAN	Up to 56 years in captivity

ANIMAL FACTS

The imperial eagle is the second-largest eagle in Europe. It is usually solitary, but during migration, eagles may form loose flocks of 10 or more birds. It feeds mainly on rabbits and ground squirrels, dropping down on prey from above. Its strong *talons* (claws) and powerful wings enable it to carry such prey home to its nest. It also can snatch birds in midflight. Juveniles are yellow-brown, with darker flight feathers and white upper-wing bars.

Imperial eagles are an impressive but increasingly rare sight in the wild, as numbers of these magnificent birds continue to fall. They have already disappeared from many parts of Europe.

WHERE IN THE WORLD?

Breeds in central Europe across Asia to Mongolia. Spends the winter in eastern Africa and southern Asia.

BILL
A powerful, curved hook at the end of the bill is used to rip and tear prey into bite-sized chunks.

WINGS
The wings are tipped with large flight feathers. These give the eagle great control during flight.

MANY THREATS

Eastern imperial eagles are seriously threatened by illegal poisonings, electrocution from flying into power lines, and the destruction of their *habitat* (living area).

FEET
The powerful clawed feet are well suited to grasping and killing prey.

HOW BIG IS IT?

Juvenile

SIBLING RIVALRY

Eagles lay their eggs several days apart. As a result, larger first-born chicks may bully or even kill smaller chicks to get more food. Imperial eagle parents try to ensure that each chick gets enough food to survive.

Northern Crested Caracara

VITAL STATISTICS

LENGTH	19-23 in (49-58 cm)
WINGSPAN	4 ft (1.2 m)
LAYS EGGS	January–March
INCUBATION PERIOD	28–32 days
FLEDGLING PERIOD	At least 56 days
NUMBER OF EGGS	2–3 eggs
NUMBER OF BROODS	1–2 a year
CALL	Mostly silent
TYPICAL DIET	Small mammals, reptiles, amphibians, and animal remains
LIFE SPAN	Unknown

ANIMAL FACTS

Although this bird of prey is sometimes called the Mexican eagle, caracaras are actually falcons. But unlike other falcons, caracaras are not especially fast flyers. They maintain large *territories* (home areas) and are spread thinly across the countryside. Caracaras are endangered, largely because much of their *habitat* (living space) has been destroyed by agriculture. Also, many caracaras are struck by automobiles as they feed on roadkill.

The northern crested caracara in flight.

According to myth, the Aztecs built their capital, Tenochtitlan, on the spot where they saw a caracara perched on a cactus, devouring a snake. Mexico City was built atop the destroyed Aztec city.

WHERE IN THE WORLD?

Lives along the border of Mexico and the United States, from Baja to eastern Texas, south to Panama. An isolated group lives in central Florida.

HEAD
A shock of short feathers, from the base of the bill to the neck gives caracaras their characteristic black crest.

FEET
Caracaras have long, strong legs. Unlike most falcons, they spend much of their time on the ground.

TAIL
The long tail has banded patterns, with alternating black and white stripes, ending in a wide black band.

HOW BIG IS IT?

MEAT THIEVES
Caracaras will eat almost anything. They are skilled hunters in their own right, but they are known for stealing food from other birds. Like vultures, they feed on *carrion* (dead and decaying animal remains).

Burrowing Owl

VITAL STATISTICS

WEIGHT	4–6 oz (0.1–0.2 kg)
LENGTH	8.5–11 in (22–28 cm)
WINGSPAN	21–22 in (53–60 cm)
SEXUAL MATURITY	1 year
LAYS EGGS	April
INCUBATION PERIOD	21–28 days
FLEDGLING PERIOD	About 28 days
NUMBER OF EGGS	3–5 eggs
NUMBER OF BROODS	1 a year
TYPICAL DIET	Small mammals, birds, and insects, especially beetles
LIFE SPAN	Up to 9 years

ANIMAL FACTS

Burrowing owls are active during the day, rather than at night like most other owls. They line their burrows with grass and roots before the female lays eggs. Males and females work together to raise their young. Young owlets can imitate the sounds made by rattlesnakes, to scare away *predators* (hunting animals). Juveniles resemble adults but lack the brown bars on their underparts. These birds are in decline, mainly because humans have destroyed much of their *habitat* (living area).

Juvenile burrowing owl

This small owl is unusual among birds for sheltering in *burrows* (underground shelters). Although it can dig its own burrow, the owl usually occupies burrows abandoned by prairie dogs or other mammals.

WHERE IN THE WORLD?

Found in western North America and the drier regions of Central and South America.

EYES
The eyes of the burrowing owl face forward, giving the bird *binocular vision* (seeing with both eyes at once). This allows the owl to judge distances more accurately.

HEAD
Forward-facing eyes offer a limited field of view. However, owls can rotate their head in a wide arc.

FEET
The burrowing owl uses its *talons* (claws) to capture prey and dig burrows.

HOW BIG IS IT?

DIGGING IN

Most owls have short legs and talons well suited to grasping prey. However, burrowing owls have long legs and long-toed feet. These are good for digging burrows. A short, furlike down covers the legs, helping to keep them free of dirt.

Rose-Colored Starling

SPECIES • *Sturnus roseus*

VITAL STATISTICS

WEIGHT	2.5 oz (78 g)
LENGTH	7.5–8.5 in (19–22 cm)
WINGSPAN	15 in (38 cm)
SEXUAL MATURITY	1 year
INCUBATION PERIOD	11–12 days
FLEDGLING PERIOD	Around 24 days
NUMBER OF EGGS	3–6 eggs
NUMBER OF BROODS	1 a year, occasionally 2
HABITS	Active at day, migratory
TYPICAL DIET	Insects in the breeding season; some fruit and berries in the winter

ANIMAL FACTS

Also known as the rosy starling, this bird breeds in large, noisy colonies. These colonies can contain as many as 100,000 breeding pairs. The location of the colonies depends on the distribution of insect prey, especially locusts. The birds are useful to farmers because they feed on these pests. Rose-colored starlings can often be seen swarming in swirling clouds over fields at dusk and dawn.

Rose-colored starling in flight

With their raucous calls and pink feathers, rose-colored starlings make a striking spectacle, whether on the ground or gathered in vast, squealing flocks.

WHERE IN THE WORLD?

Spends the summer in eastern Europe into mild areas of Asia. Winters in tropical southern Asia.

SONG
The song of the rose-colored starling includes whistles, squeaks, warbles, and grating noises.

BODY
Although the body of these birds is pink, the amount of red tinting on the feathers varies from bird to bird.

HEAD
Male rose-colored starlings have a longer head crest than females. The crest is raised during courtship displays.

FEET
The feet and long toes of rose-colored starlings are typical of perching birds.

HOW BIG IS IT?

EARLY BLOOMERS

Rose-colored starlings rely on locusts and other insects to feed their young. These insects are abundant for only a limited time. As a result, the eggs of these birds incubate for a relatively short time, and the chicks can soon fly.

Spinifexbird

VITAL STATISTICS

LENGTH	6 in (15 cm)
SEXUAL MATURITY	Possibly 1 year
INCUBATION PERIOD	Uncertain
FLEDGLING PERIOD	Uncertain
NUMBER OF EGGS	2 eggs
NUMBER OF BROODS	Uncertain
CALL	Males make a short, melodic "je-swee-a-voo" cry
HABITS	Active in day, nonmigratory
TYPICAL DIET	Insects and spiders; occasional seeds
LIFE SPAN	Unknown

ANIMAL FACTS

Spinifexbirds belong to a group of perching birds known as warblers. Spinifexbirds live among tall grasses in dry grasslands. Although their numbers remain healthy, these birds are in decline in some areas because of introduced *predators* (hunting animals), particularly rats and cats, and frequent brush fires.

Mystery surrounds the Australian spinifexbird. Hidden away in thickets of prickly spinifex grass, this little bird is rarely seen. Usually, the only sign of its presence is the bird's distinct, melodic cry.

WHERE IN THE WORLD?

Spinifexbirds are found only in Australia, throughout the northern interior. Their preferred habitat is spinifex, or porcupine grass.

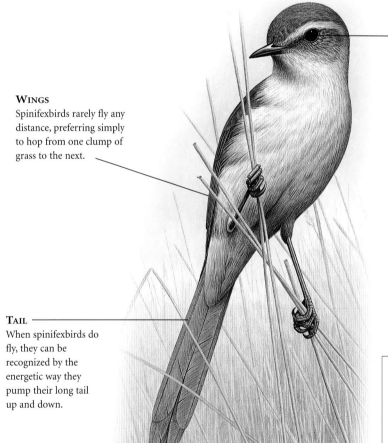

EYES
Eyes on the side of the head give a wide field of vision, which helps the spinifexbird spot danger more easily.

WINGS
Spinifexbirds rarely fly any distance, preferring simply to hop from one clump of grass to the next.

TAIL
When spinifexbirds do fly, they can be recognized by the energetic way they pump their long tail up and down.

Spinifex bird in flight

HOW BIG IS IT?

TIGHTROPE WALKERS
Long legs and strong feet enable the spinifexbird to perch and walk with ease among swaying stems of spinifex grass. The long tail acts like a tightrope-walker's pole, helping the bird to maintain its balance as it leaps from stem to stem.

Budgerigar

VITAL STATISTICS

WEIGHT	0.7–1.2 oz (20–35 g)
LENGTH	6.7–7.5 in (17–19 cm)
WINGSPAN	12–14 in (30–35 cm)
NUMBER OF EGGS	4–6 eggs
INCUBATION PERIOD	18–21 days
NUMBER OF BROODS	2–3 a year
TYPICAL DIET	Seeds, nuts, fruits, berries
LIFE SPAN	Up to 10 years

The budgerigar is among the smallest of all parrots, which partly explains why it has become a popular pet. It is often called the common parakeet or "budgie."

WHERE IN THE WORLD?

Found across the interior of the Australian continent in grasslands and scrubland. Introduced populations thrive in the southern United States.

ANIMAL FACTS

Budgerigars are highly social animals that gather in large flocks that feed together. The flock provides protection from *predators* (hunting animals) by bringing together many sets of eyes to watch for danger. Members of the flock communicate using loud calls. The loud calls of pet budgerigars can make them a bothersome pet. The pets have been bred in a variety of colors and patterns. However, the wild budgerigar has a yellow forehead and face, with a blue or purple cheek patch and three black spots across the throat. The breast and belly are green. The tail is cobalt-blue.

HEAD
The wild budgerigar has fewer puffy head feathers than the most common type of pet budgerigar.

POLLY WANT A CRACKER?
Most budgies can be trained to talk by saying the same word over and over again to them until the budgie repeats it. It is best to start when the bird is only a few weeks old. Both the male and the female can learn many words.

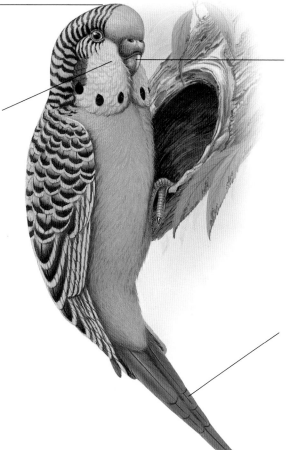

BILL
The upper, hooked part of the bill is attached to the skull by a hinge that allows the bill to move up and down.

TAIL
The tail is used both for steering in the air and displaying to other budgerigars.

Female (left), male (right)

HOW BIG IS IT?

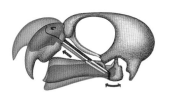

CHEWING IT OVER

The budgerigar is an intelligent bird that often investigates objects with its bill. This bill is unusual among birds in its ability to move up and down because of a hinge in the skull.

Great Bustard

VITAL STATISTICS

WEIGHT	Males: 17.5–45 lb (8–20 kg) Females: 7.7–11 lb (3.5–5 kg)
LENGTH	Males: 35.5–39 in (90–100 cm). Females: 29.5–33.5 in (75–85 cm)
WINGSPAN	Males: 7–8 ft (2.1–2.4 m). Females: 5.6–6.2 ft (1.7–2m)
SEXUAL MATURITY	Males: Around 5 years
LAYS EGGS	Breeding begins in March
INCUBATION PERIOD	Around 28 days
NUMBER OF EGGS	2–3 eggs
NUMBER OF BROODS	1 per nest but males may mate with up to 5 females
TYPICAL DIET	Plants, insects, and other small animals
LIFE SPAN	10 years

ANIMAL FACTS

Male great bustards put on a flamboyant display when the breeding season arrives. Their plumage becomes brighter and they puff themselves up, flashing their white underparts to attract the attention of potential mates.

Male great bustard

Male great bustards are the heaviest birds capable of flight. Unfortunately, the number of these birds has fallen sharply, mainly because their *habitat* (living area) has been taken over for agriculture.

WHERE IN THE WORLD?

Breeds in southern and central Europe, along with mild parts of Asia. The European birds tend to be permanent residents, while the Asian birds migrate south for the winter.

HEAD
During the breeding season, male great bustards grow a large beard, which can reach 8 inches (20 centimeters) in length.

WINGS
Despite their size, great bustards are fast fliers, using their powerful wings to reach speeds of up to 37 miles (60 kilometers) per hour.

BODY
Bustards have a huge difference in size between the sexes. Some males are 50 percent as large as females.

HOW BIG IS IT?

HIDDEN IN THE GRASS

The scarcity of trees in grasslands forces many birds to build their nests on the ground. As a result, eggs and chicks are vulnerable to many different *predators* (hunting animals). Like most other ground-nesting birds, great bustards rely on camouflage to keep their eggs and chicks hidden.

Greater Prairie Chicken

SPECIES • *Tympanuchus cupido*

Male greater prairie chickens attract a harem of females with their elaborate mating dances and dramatic display feathers. These rare and beautiful birds are not closely related to domestic chickens.

VITAL STATISTICS

WEIGHT	1.5–2.6 lb (0.7–1.2 kg)
LENGTH	18.5 in (47 cm)
SEXUAL MATURITY	1 year
LAYS EGGS	Breeding starts late March
INCUBATION PERIOD	23–24 days
NUMBER OF EGGS	5–17 eggs
NUMBER OF BROODS	1 per nest, but males mate with many females
CALL	Male makes booming "whooo-doo-dooh"
TYPICAL DIET	Seeds, fruit, and insects
LIFE SPAN	Typically 2–3 years

WHERE IN THE WORLD?

Once common throughout North American grasslands, this bird now survives only in isolated areas.

ANIMAL FACTS

Greater prairie chickens are rugged birds that stay in grasslands all year. They have no trouble surviving harsh winter weather and even use heavy snow like an insulating blanket. Unfortunately, wild fires and flash floods kill many chicks in the spring and summer. As with other grassland animals, agriculture has greatly damaged the *habitat* (living area) of these birds. Their numbers have fallen dramatically.

Mother and brood

HEAD —
Adult females have shorter head feathers and lack the males' orange eyebrows and the circular patches on the neck.

"EARS"
During breeding displays, males raise their elongated, earlike feathers above their heads, to look more impressive to mates.

NECK
Large orange patches on the side of the male prairie chicken's neck are inflated during breeding displays.

HOW BIG IS IT?

COCK OF THE WALK

Among prairie chickens, a small number of males mates with many females. Males gather together on breeding grounds with little grass. Males strut and flash their colorful feathers to attract females. Males that make the most impressive displays win most of the females.

Gray Partridge

VITAL STATISTICS

WEIGHT	10.6–16 oz (300–450 g)
LENGTH	11.0–12.6 in (28–32 cm)
WINGSPAN	17.3–21.7 in (44–55 cm)
NUMBER OF EGGS	10–20 eggs (up to 29)
INCUBATION PERIOD	23–25 days
NUMBER OF BROODS	1 a year
TYPICAL DIET	Seeds, shoots, leaves, and also insects, grubs, and worms
LIFE SPAN	Up to 10 years

The gray partridge is a hardy grassland bird that has long been popular with hunters. When threatened, it usually flies only a short distance, like many other ground-nesting birds.

WHERE IN THE WORLD?

Found in Europe extending into central Russia, but is absent from most of the Iberian Peninsula and northern Scandinavia. It has been introduced into North America.

ANIMAL FACTS

The gray partridge has been a favorite *game bird* (bird hunted for sport or food) for centuries. A native of Eurasia, it has been introduced into many foreign grasslands. These include the grasslands of North America, where it has thrived. It is especially successful in northern areas of the continent, where it is often known as the Hungarian partridge. The gray partridge is better at coping with *habitat* (living area) destruction caused by agriculture than many other ground-nesting birds. It often nests in fields of winter wheat. Juveniles are yellow-brown.

Juvenile

BILL
A short, slightly curved bill is used for picking up seeds and tearing off leaves.

WINGS
Short round wings give the bird a powerful but rather uneven flight.

LEGS
Short legs and stout feet are well adapted for scratching in the ground after food.

HOW BIG IS IT?

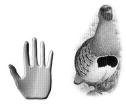

GRUBBING ON GRUBS

Gray partridge females typically lay 10 to 20 eggs in a ground nest. After about three weeks, the chicks hatch. Although adults eat mostly seeds, chicks feed only on insects for the first week after they hatch. The parents lead them to areas with abundant insects where they can get a good meal.

Southern Ground Hornbill

SPECIES • *Bucorvus leadbeateri*

This stately bird is the largest species of hornbill. The southern ground hornbill is declining in numbers and is now limited mainly to national parks.

VITAL STATISTICS

WEIGHT	Males: 7 to 14 lb (3.2–6.2 kg) Females: 5 to 10 lb (2.2–4.6 kg)
LENGTH	3–4.5 ft (0.9–1.3 m)
WINGSPAN	1.5–2 ft (0.5–0.6 m)
SEXUAL MATURITY	4 years
LAYS EGGS	October–November
INCUBATION PERIOD	40–42 days
NUMBER OF EGGS	2 eggs
NUMBER OF BROODS	1 a year
TYPICAL DIET	Mammals, reptiles, and insects
LIFE SPAN	Up to 40 years

ANIMAL FACTS

Southern ground hornbills favor relatively dry grasslands and savannas. They often live in groups of 5 to 10 individuals. These groups guard their *territory* (home area) from other hornbills. The birds may follow herds of grazing animals to feed on animals flushed from cover by the herd. Juveniles are known to playfully wrestle using their bills. This behavior may provide training in use of the bill to attack prey.

WHERE IN THE WORLD?

Found in southern Africa, in Namibia, Angola, South Africa, Burundi, and Kenya.

MOVEABLE FEAST
Southern ground hornbills often collect a number of insects and other prey animals and may carry them around in their bill for some time before swallowing them all at once.

NECK
Hornbills have an extra neckbone, which makes it easier for them to grab prey on the ground.

WINGS
Long white, fingerlike primary feathers are used in mating displays. They provide a startling contrast to the black feathers of these birds.

FEET
Southern ground hornbills can fly, but they spend most of their time on the ground, walking with a slow, stately gait.

HOW BIG IS IT?

DEADLY BILL
A huge bill, hinged by powerful muscles, enables the southern ground hornbill to feed on a wide variety of small animals. They grab and quickly subdue even dangerous snakes. They also can feed on mammals as large as hares.

Emu

VITAL STATISTICS

WEIGHT	66–132.5 lb (30–60 kg)
LENGTH	3.5 ft (2 m)
HEIGHT	5.5 ft (1.7 m)
SEXUAL MATURITY	2–3 year
LAYS EGGS	May–June
NUMBER OF EGGS	5–15 eggs
INCUBATION PERIOD	52–60 days
TYPICAL DIET	Plants, fruit, seeds, insects
LIFE SPAN	From 10–20 years

The flightless emu is the second-largest bird, surpassed only by the ostrich. More than 600 places in Australia are named after these majestic birds.

WHERE IN THE WORLD?

Found in most parts of Australia, especially the interior.

ANIMAL FACTS

It is the male emu that has a mothering instinct. A single female may lay eggs for several males. The males then *incubate* (sit on) the eggs, going without food and water. After the eggs hatch, the emu chicks are able to move around and feed within a few days. Still, the males stay with them for about six months, teaching them how to look after themselves. Male emus with chicks may attack people that come too close. Emus are solitary by nature but sometimes form large flocks where food is abundant.

LOWER BODY
The pelvic muscles of the emu are large and powerful, giving it a large stride and a mighty kick.

FEET
The emu has only three large toes. This adaptation is common among birds that spend their time walking and running.

WINGS
The emu cannot fly and has only tiny wings. However, it runs at up to about 35 miles (56 kilometers) per hour, which enables it to speed away from *predators* (hunting animals).

STAYING COOL
By lifting its wings, the bird exposes a network of veins close to the skin. This helps the bird to cool down.

Juvenile

HOW BIG IS IT?

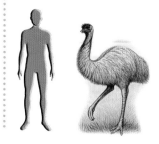

FEATHERS

To stay cool in the baking Australian sun, the emu has loose, hairlike feathers. These feathers allow heat to escape more quickly than conventionally shaped feathers. Each emu feather has two plumes connected to a single base.

Greater Rhea

The greater rhea is South America's version of the emu. It is not as big as its Australian counterpart, but it is just as feisty. Unfortunately, its numbers are in decline because of *habitat* (living space) destruction.

VITAL STATISTICS

WEIGHT	50.5 lb (23 kg)
HEIGHT	4.5 ft (1.4 m)
SEXUAL MATURITY	2 years
LAYS EGGS	August–January, depending on location
INCUBATION PERIOD	35–40 days
NUMBER OF EGGS	Up to 60 eggs
NUMBER OF BROODS	Males court up to 12 females, who all lay eggs in his nest. He incubates up to 60 eggs at a time.
HABITS	Active in day, nonmigratory
TYPICAL DIET	Plants, small insects, and reptiles
LIFE SPAN	Up to 40 years

ANIMAL FACTS

The greater rhea prefers areas with tall grasses, such as pampas grass. During the summer, males are solitary, while females live in small groups. During the winter, males, females, and chicks form large flocks. As with emus, rhea males build the nests and provide care for chicks. Females lay eggs in many different nests.

Female greater rhea

WHERE IN THE WORLD?

Lives in the grasslands of South America, especially Argentina. Also farmed in North America and Europe.

BEACH BIRDS
Rhea often live in brush-covered land near water where they can bathe and swim.

NECK
The long, flexible neck sweeps the ground, in search of both plants and insects to eat.

FEET
With three sturdy toes, the feet of a greater rhea are more like those of a grazing animal than a bird.

BODY AND LEGS
Meat from the muscular body and legs of the bird have made it attractive for ranching. The eggs and feathers are also valuable.

HOW BIG IS IT?

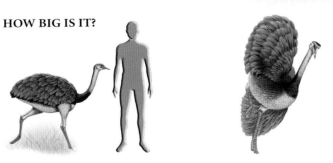

WINGING IT
The greater rhea has unusually long wings for a flightless bird. It uses these wings to help it maneuver on the run. The wings help the bird to keep its balance and steer, by lifting one and then the other. In this way, the wing acts like the rudder on an airplane.

Slowworm

VITAL STATISTICS

WEIGHT	0.7–3.5 oz (20–100 g); males are smaller
LENGTH	12–20 in (30–50 cm)
SEXUAL MATURITY	3 years, based on growth rate; maturity is related to body size, rather than age
GESTATION PERIOD	3–5 months
NUMBER OF OFFSPRING	6–12 live young; can be up to 26
DIET	Earthworms, insects, slugs, and spiders
LIFE SPAN	20 years

Also known as the blindworm, the slowworm may look like a snake, but it is actually a legless lizard. Unlike a snake, it has eyelids and can blink. Snakes have a clear scale that covers and protects the eye.

WHERE IN THE WORLD?

Widely distributed throughout Europe but absent from the far north and Spain. Extends into northwestern Asia.

ANIMAL FACTS

Most scientists believe that snakes developed from *burrowing* (digging) lizards that looked much like the slowworm. Slowworms live in a range of *habitats* (areas). They frequently visit gardens to find prey. Sometimes, they burrow into compost heaps. Young slowworms develop in eggs that remain within the mother's body. They hatch before they are born. Their coloration is variable. Some are silvery-gray, with prominent black markings down the flanks. Others are brown to red.

APPEARANCE
A dark stripe runs down the center of the back, but males lose this marking as they mature.

COLORATION
Adults can range from brown to red to gray.

HEAD
The head merges directly into the body. The scales here, as elsewhere, are very small.

DEFENSIVE REACTION
If a slowworm is threatened, its tail will detach with hardly any bleeding. The tail will twitch on the ground, attracting the attention of the *predator* (hunting animal). This allows the slowworm to slip away unnoticed. Afterward, the slowworm *regenerates* (regrows) a new tail.

Slowworms hibernate over the winter, emerging in March.

HOW BIG IS IT?

SHEDDING
Slowworms shed their skins as they grow. The skin comes off the body as a thin, semitransparent casing.

Gopher Tortoise

VITAL STATISTICS

WEIGHT	9 lb (4.1 kg)
LENGTH	About 10 in (25 cm) over the central part of the shell
SEXUAL MATURITY	10–15 years
NUMBER OF EGGS	3–15; young resemble miniature adults
INCUBATION PERIOD	70–100 days, depending on temperature
DIET	Feeds mainly on plants such as wiregrass; also eats fruit and berries; occasionally animal remains
LIFE SPAN	40–60 years

ANIMAL FACTS

The gopher tortoise and its relatives are the only group of tortoises native to North America. The tortoise's remarkable burrows can be up to 40 feet (12 meters) long. There is a single entrance, with the tunnel dug so the tortoise can turn around within it. The burrows provide protection from harsh weather and *predators* (hunting animals). The gopher tortoise is threatened, mostly by hunting and the destruction of its *habitat* (place where an animal lives). Fire ants are another threat. This invasive species feeds on the tortoise's eggs. The gopher tortoise's decline also threatens the many animals that use its burrows.

The gopher tortoise gets its name from the long *burrows* (underground shelters) it digs. Other animals also use these burrows. Thus, the tortoise is a "keystone species," on which many other animals depend.

WHERE IN THE WORLD?

Lives in southeastern parts of the United States, ranging from southeastern South Carolina to Florida and along the Gulf of Mexico.

A TURTLE BY ANOTHER NAME
A tortoise is a turtle that lives only on land.

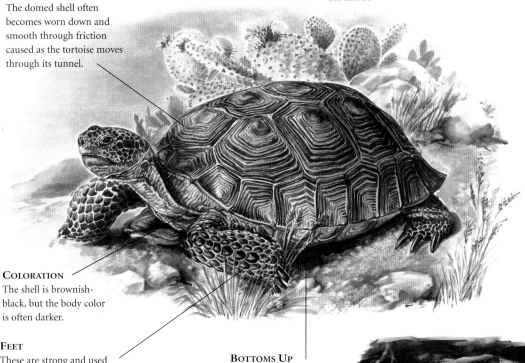

SHELL
The domed shell often becomes worn down and smooth through friction caused as the tortoise moves through its tunnel.

COLORATION
The shell is brownish-black, but the body color is often darker.

FEET
These are strong and used for digging burrows as well as shoveling soil.

BOTTOMS UP
The underside of the shell, called the plastron, is concave in adult males. In females, the plastron is flat.

HOW BIG IS IT?

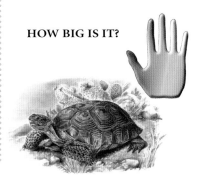

BURROWS
Other species use the burrows made by these tortoises, including burrowing owls, frogs, insects, mice, and snakes.

Moor Frog

VITAL STATISTICS

LENGTH	1.8–2.5 in (4–6.5 cm)
SEXUAL MATURITY	2–5 years; females are generally slower to mature
HATCHING PERIOD	2–3 weeks, depending on the water temperature
NUMBER OF EGGS	1,000–2,000 laid between March and April
HABITAT	Typically moorland areas, with swamps and ponds
DIET	Mainly insects and other small animals
LIFE SPAN	Up to 11 years

ANIMAL FACTS

The moor frog lives in a variety of *habitats* (living areas) but is especially common in open country with boggy ground. A "moor" is an open area with wet soil and many shallow pools. The frog can also be found in meadows and gardens. When threatened, a moor frog takes a giant leap and then digs into the soil to escape. Moor frogs *hibernate* (enter a sleeplike state) during the winter. These frogs remain abundant, but they are at risk from water pollution, which harms eggs and *tadpoles* (immature frogs).

White underside of the body

The breeding grounds of this *species* (kind) of frog come alive in the spring, with hundreds of male frogs singing to attract females. The eggs are laid in shallow, stagnant water.

WHERE IN THE WORLD?

Lives in northern and eastern Europe, extending across much of northern Asia.

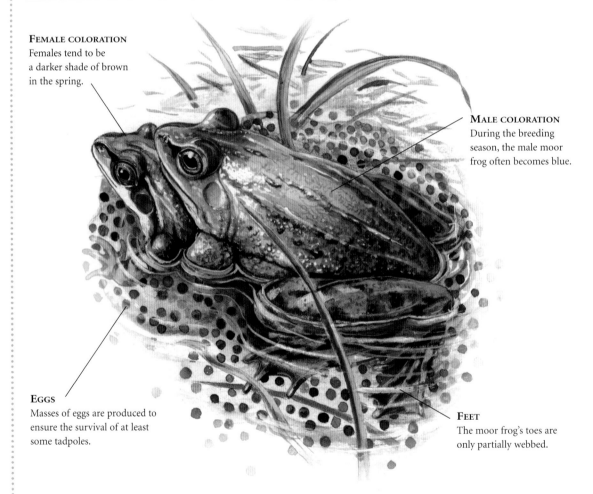

FEMALE COLORATION
Females tend to be a darker shade of brown in the spring.

MALE COLORATION
During the breeding season, the male moor frog often becomes blue.

EGGS
Masses of eggs are produced to ensure the survival of at least some tadpoles.

FEET
The moor frog's toes are only partially webbed.

HOW BIG IS IT?

COMMUNITY CHORUS

Huge numbers of these frogs may gather in areas of shallow, stagnant water, which are good for laying eggs. Males sing to attract mates.

Great Green Bush Cricket

SPECIES · *Tettigonia viridissima*

VITAL STATISTICS

LENGTH	Up to 2 in (5 cm)
SEXUAL MATURITY	Eggs hatch in the year after being laid or the year after that; young pass through six stages
EGGS	Several hundred
DEVELOPMENTAL PERIOD	Up to 3 years, depending on when the young hatch
HABITAT	Grasslands and edges of woodland
DIET	Hunts caterpillars, moths, and flies, but also eats vegetation
LIFE SPAN	6 months

ANIMAL FACTS

Male crickets attract females with loud songs. However, these songs do not come from the mouth. Rather, males sing by rubbing their rigid forewings together. The song is so loud that it can be heard at least 165 feet (50 meters) away. Although they sing during the day, bush crickets tend to be noisier at dusk, into the evening. Females may also communicate with similar sounds during the breeding period. The female plants her eggs in the soil using a long, thin organ called an ovipositor. Unlike many other insects, young crickets look much like the adults.

Females lay eggs in the soil.

This is one of the largest and loudest crickets found in grasslands. Like other crickets, it can be distinguished from grasshoppers by its long antennae. These reach three times the length of the body.

WHERE IN THE WORLD?

Lives throughout much of Europe, extending through Turkey into Asia. Also present in North Africa.

FEET
Hooks at the ends of the legs help the bush cricket hold on to strands of grass.

SPINES
Sharp projections on the lower part of the bush cricket's legs provide some protection against *predators* (hunting animals).

APPETITE
Although the crickets may feed on crops, they help farmers by eating many harmful insects.

THORAX
A broad shield covers the middle part of the insect's body, with a red stripe down its center.

COLORATION
These crickets are mainly an attractive lime-green, with faint red markings.

IN FLIGHT
The broader, transparent hindwings are usually concealed beneath the rugged forewings.

HOW BIG IS IT?

Field Cricket

VITAL STATISTICS

LENGTH	0.6–1.0 in (1.7–2.5 cm); males slightly larger
SEXUAL MATURITY	Young crickets overwinter in burrows as nymphs, maturing the following year
EGGS	About 5 eggs daily, around 70–100 in all
DEVELOPMENTAL PERIOD	Adults start breeding in May; nymphs hatch in July and August
HABITAT	Dry, sunny localities with well-drained soil
DIET	Mainly grass, but also eats animal remains
LIFE SPAN	Up to 1 year

ANIMAL FACTS

This *species* (kind) of field crickets has declined mainly because of *habitat* (living area) destruction caused by agriculture. The London Zoo has organized a conservation effort aimed at restoring the cricket to areas of England where it has disappeared. The crickets are bred in captivity and then set free. The first batch was released in an area of West Sussex. Several thousand others have followed at various protected locations. Similar field crickets are found throughout much of the world.

These crickets prefer sunny places where the grass and other vegetation is short. They have declined dramatically in recent years, particularly in England. Work is underway to prevent their extinction.

WHERE IN THE WORLD?

Found in southern and central Europe, as far north as Germany and the Netherlands. Survives in parts of England.

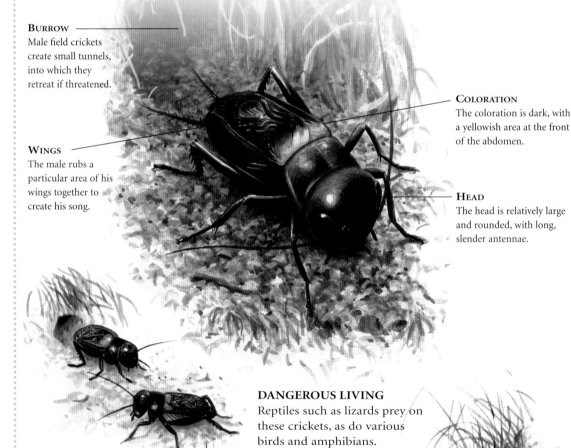

BURROW
Male field crickets create small tunnels, into which they retreat if threatened.

WINGS
The male rubs a particular area of his wings together to create his song.

COLORATION
The coloration is dark, with a yellowish area at the front of the abdomen.

HEAD
The head is relatively large and rounded, with long, slender antennae.

DANGEROUS LIVING
Reptiles such as lizards prey on these crickets, as do various birds and amphibians.

HOW BIG IS IT?

ATTRACTING A MATE
The male cricket chirps from the mouth of his burrow throughout the day, in the hope of attracting a mate.

Buff-Tailed Bumblebee

SPECIES • *Bombus terrestris*

These bees are common in Europe and some countries in Asia. However, the bees are banned from the United States and Canada because of concerns that they would threaten native bee *species* (kinds).

VITAL STATISTICS

LENGTH	Workers 0.6–0.8 in (1.5–2 cm); queen up to 1.1 in (2.7 cm)
SEXUAL MATURITY	Males within a few weeks; queens by a year old
NUMBER OF EGGS	Perhaps 1,000, laid by the queen
DEVELOPMENTAL PERIOD	5 weeks from *larva* (young) to worker bee
HABITAT	Open country with flowering plants nearby
DIET	Pollen and nectar from flowers
LIFE SPAN	Queens 1 year; workers a few weeks

WHERE IN THE WORLD?

Can be found throughout most of Europe. Introduced to Japan, New Zealand, and mainland Asia.

ANIMAL FACTS

Queens emerge from their *hibernation* (sleeplike state) early in the year to build a nest. They then lay eggs that hatch to become female workers. These workers quickly build up the colony, making frequent trips to find nectar and pollen made by flowers. The queen only produces males in the later summer. The males leave the nest to find young queens. The males die shortly after they mate. The new queens will find somewhere snug to hibernate before winter.

The front legs (right) are more streamlined than the hind legs (left), helping the bee to fly.

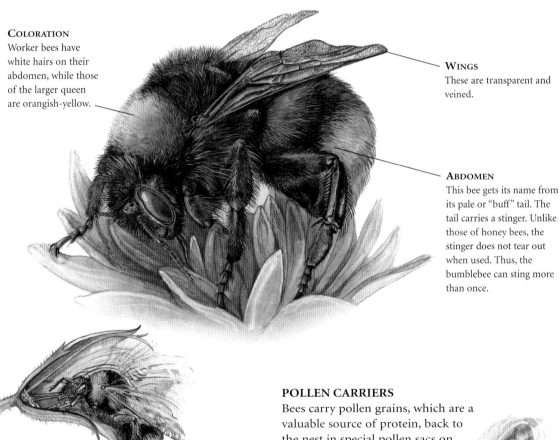

COLORATION
Worker bees have white hairs on their abdomen, while those of the larger queen are orangish-yellow.

WINGS
These are transparent and veined.

ABDOMEN
This bee gets its name from its pale or "buff" tail. The tail carries a stinger. Unlike those of honey bees, the stinger does not tear out when used. Thus, the bumblebee can sting more than once.

POLLEN CARRIERS
Bees carry pollen grains, which are a valuable source of protein, back to the nest in special pollen sacs on their hind legs.

HOW BIG IS IT?

BEARING FRUIT
Workers are responsible for collecting nectar and pollen. While doing so, they fertilize the flowers.

Glossary

adaptation a characteristic of a living thing that makes it better able to survive and reproduce in its environment

binocular vision seeing with both eyes at once

boom-and-bust cycle an ecological cycle during which a species greatly increases in numbers and then crashes to low numbers again

burrow underground shelter

carrion dead and decaying animal flesh

domesticate to change an animal or plant from a wild to a tame state suitable for agriculture

dominance hierarchy a ranking of individuals by their influence in relation to each other

ecosystem a group of animal and plant populations living together in the same environment and its *abiotic* (nonliving or physical) environment, including climate, soil, water, air, nutrients, and energy

grassland a region with mostly grass and few trees that is one of the four chief kinds of natural vegetation (along with forests, desert shrubs, and tundras); most grasslands lie between very arid lands, or deserts, and humid lands covered with forests, though some grasslands occur in humid climates

habitat the kind of place in which an animal lives

hibernation an inactive, sleeplike state that some animals enter during the winter

incisor a tooth having a sharp edge for cutting

keystone species a plant or animal species necessary to the survival of an ecosystem

mammal an animal that feeds its young on the mother's milk

moor a large open area with wet soil and many shallow pools

nectar a sugary liquid that is produced by flowering plants

nymph any one of certain insects in the stage of development between egg and adult

pack a number of animals of the same kind hunting or living together

Pampas steepes in Argentina

plastron the part of a turtle's shell that covers the belly

pollen tiny grains that are produced in the male organs of flowering and cone-bearing plants; seeds develop after pollen is transferred from the male part of a plant to the female part

prairie a tall-grass grasslands in a relatively humid climate, with a thick cover of grasses and, often, patches of forests. Large prairies include much of the American Midwest, the Pampas of eastern Argentina, and parts of Hungary and northeastern China.

predator an animal that preys upon other animals

regeneration in plants and animals, the capacity to replace lost or damaged parts by growing new ones

rodent a type of mammal with front teeth especially suited to gnawing hard objects

scrubland land overgrown with low, stunted trees or shrubs

species a kind of living thing; members of a species share many characteristics and are able to interbreed

steepe a semiarid grassland, with scattered bunches of short grasses in the driest parts and taller, more closely spaced grasses in the more humid parts. Well-known steppes include the Great Plains of North America, the western part of the Pampas of Argentina, and the veld of South Africa.

tadpole a water-dwelling, immature frog or toad, also called polliwog

talon the claw of an animal, especially a bird of prey

territory an area within definite boundaries, such as a nesting ground, in which an animal lives and from which it keeps out others of its kind

thermal a rising current of warm air

thorax the part of the body between the base of the neck and the abdomen, also called the chest

veld a steepe in South Africa

wean to accustom a young animal to food other than its mother's milk

Resources

Books

Animals on the Trail with Lewis and Clark
by Dorothy Hinshaw Patent and William Muñoz
(Clarion Books, 2002) Follow the path across the North
American grasslands taken by Lewis and Clark's famous
expedition and learn about the animals they found
along the way.

Grasslands and Deserts by Gail Radley and Jean Sherlock
(Carolrhoda Books, 2001) In this volume of the
"Disappearing From"series, poems and short essays sit
alongside scientific information about the wildlife of
grasslands and deserts.

Life in the Temperate Grasslands by Laurie Toupin
(Franklin Watts, 2005) Learn more about the plants
and animals that inhabit the world's grassland biomes,
from the North American prairies to the African velds.

Websites

Grassland: Terrain of Many Names
http://environment.nationalgeographic.com/
environment/habitats/grassland
This website from National Geographic takes a look at
grasslands around the world and explores the threats
facing these habitats.

What's It Like Where You Live? Grassland
http://www.mbgnet.net/sets/grasslnd/
This website from the Missouri Botanical Garden in St.
Louis answers many of the most common questions
people have about prairie grasslands.

Grassland Animals
http://www.nature.org/newsfeatures/specialfeatures/
animals/grassland-animals.xml
Learn about the fight to protect the animals of Earth's
grasslands at this website created by the Nature
Conservancy.

Acknowledgments

Cover photograph: Alamy (Juniors Bildarchiv)

Illustrations: © Art-Tech

Photographs:

Ardea: 32 (D. Hadden)

Corbis RF: 9, 10, 12, 25

Dreamstime: 6 (E. Isselee), 17 (M. Pawinski),
20 (N. Paklina), 24 (W. Overman), 34 (A. Huszti),
36 (J. Gottwald), 39 (S. Ekernas), 41 (P. Watson)

FLPA: 7 (Frank Lane), 13 (T. Whittaker), 15 (Frans
Lanting), 21 (Foto Natura), 26 (David Hosking),
34 (S.D.K. Maslowski), 42 (W. Wisniewski), 44 (Panda
Photo), 45 (F. Merlet)

T. Friedel: 30

iStock Photo: 40 (M. Divis)

Morguefile: 27 (Matthew Hull)

Photos.com: 14, 18, 19, 35, 43

Public Domain: 29, 33, 38

SuperStock: 16 (NHPA), 22 (Animals Animals),
31 (imagebroker)

M. Trischler: 28

Webshots: 9 (B. Chloe), 11 (C. Hitchcock)

Index